Presenting Stefano della Bella

Presenting Stefano della Bella

Seventeenth - century Printmaker

by Phyllis Dearborn Massar

The Metropolitan Museum of Art

Distributed by New York Graphic Society

Designed by Peter Oldenburg
Type set by Finn Typographic Service, Inc.
Printed by The Meriden Gravure Company
Bound by Tapley-Rutter Company, Inc.

Contents

Introduction

The artist would need no introduction to most people were this the seventeenth or the eighteenth century. Seventeenth-century city dwellers bought prints as casually as we today buy post cards and weekly magazines, and Stefano della Bella's were particularly popular. Eighteenth-century collectors competitively filled cabinets and scrapbooks with the thousand-odd Della Bella etchings, minute to large, and artists, too, owned many of them as a source for people, animals, or ornament motifs for their own work.

Rather neglected in the nineteenth century—tastes had changed—Della Bella's prints were seldom listed in dealers' catalogues in the first half of the twentieth, for they were considered too cheap and plentiful to bother with. A narrowing market has lately brought Della Bella into focus as an artist, and his prints are again esteemed for their virtuosity and delicacy of technique as well as for their diverse and often amusing subjects. Technically, Stefano was a master of shading, exquisitely small details, and the rendering of fur and feathers.

The prints have a broad interest when they are considered as reflections of the artist's life and times. Working with his sketchbook and etching needle much the way today's magazine photographer works with his camera, Stefano was on the spot for some notable events and developments of the turbulent seventeenth century: the lavish court festivals of the Medici at Florence, the burgeoning of baroque architecture and painting in Rome (which influenced his work), the emergence of Paris as the political and cultural capital of Europe, and campaigns of the Thirty Years' War.

He was born in Florence in 1610. The premature death of his sculptor father necessitated an art apprenticeship for the boy. First trained in a goldsmith's shop, he showed such ability as a draughtsman that he was sent instead to a painter's studio. Baldinucci, the contemporary Florentine biographer of artists, says of him then, "Stefano, for his tender age of about thirteen, and for the elegance of his bearing, was called, as an endearment, by the name of Stefanino."

The young artist undertook to emulate Jacques Callot, who had enjoyed years of Medici patronage. He diligently made pen drawings after Callot's technically superb prints and was instructed in etching by Remigo Cantagallina, Callot's teacher. Stefano also began a lifelong habit of sketching out of doors, Florentine theatricals, festivals, tournaments, and hunting parties providing subject matter for his early efforts.

One of his first tries at a publishable etching was the print in the Callot manner shown in part on pages 14–15 of this book. With possible patronage in mind he dedicated it to "His Most Serene Highness the Great Prince Gian Carlo Medici," who was then sixteen. The strategy worked. Stefano began to get official Medici commissions, notably a series of book illustrations.

Rome was the magnet for an ambitious young artist in the 1620s and 30s. Under the aegis of Pope Urban VIII a great rebuilding was occurring there, transforming the ancient city into an exuberant, festive world capital. Architects of the Italian baroque were at work. Artists from France and the Netherlands were flocking there to study, to find commissions, to paint, and to make prints for the growing market of visiting travelers and pilgrims. In his twenty-third year Stefano obtained from his patron Lorenzo de' Medici, brother of the Grand Duke, permission to go to Rome, a monthly stipend as well, and a billet at the Medici palace there.

The pretext for going to Rome was to perfect himself as an artist. Judging from the evidence—at least one intact sketchbook and many single-sheet drawings are in the collections of the Uffizi, the Louvre, the Albertina, the British Museum, and at Windsor Castle—Stefano avoided studios and the study of other artists' work and spent as much time as he could drawing in the open. He frequented the Forum and areas of the city where palatial garden villas were rising, also the Campagna, where he could ride horseback and sketch ruins. Later he mined his sketchbooks for figures and backgrounds for his prints.

Perhaps it was the open-air practice that freed Stefano from the influence of the tightly technical Callot style, with its mannerist posing of figures. In any case it was during his Roman days that the true Della Bella style emerged—relaxed, almost lyrical, with figures disposed naturally rather than stagily.

Rome, finally, was not enough. Perhaps lured by the prospect of greater personal profit from the many print publishers in Paris, perhaps recalling Callot's success there, Della Bella went to Paris in 1639 with the entourage of a special ambassador, Alessandro del Nero.

His work was already known in Paris. In fact, the busy French etcher Collignon, to supply demand, had copied a set of Stefano's marines. For some time, it appears, Stefano enjoyed himself in Paris as a tourist. When at last he needed money he had no trouble finding free-lance work with the leading print publishers. Pushed by these men, he became enormously productive. Etchings in series and singles, large and small, to suit many tastes and purposes, seemed to pour from him. There were sets devoted to the military arts, landscapes, marines, animals, ornament plates, frontispieces, illustrations of theater productions, religious subjects, and many sets of capricci—vignettes of various people and countries. There were views of the new town-planning successes: the Place Dauphine and the Place Royale. There were series of Principles of Drawing: how to produce heads à la Della Bella in twenty-five lessons. And there were 199 miniature etchings for the four sets of cards that instructed the seven-year-old king, Louis XIV, in geography, mythology, and history. And, as always, Della Bella drew outdoors, supplementing his sketchbooks of Italian views and Roman ruins with drawings of French parks, Parisian strollers, horsemanship schools, and the beggars and gypsies he encountered on the roads.

Beyond this new subject matter, Della Bella now found stimulation in the work of other printmakers. Documentary evidence exists that he bought or traded his work for these prints, including some by Rembrandt. And indeed there are Della Bella prints, such as a series of heads in Oriental headdress, that show a debt to Rembrandt. But more evident is his study of landscape prints by the Dutch painter-etchers Herman van Swanevelt and Jan Both. Stefano adopted some of their techniques and in his later landscapes tried for more painterly effects, inventing contrasting textures for his trees, large-leaf plants, grass, and skies.

Della Bella knew such success in Paris that he might have remained there, but in 1648 violent demonstrations began over the taxation and financial policies of Prime Minister Mazarin, Richelieu's Italian-born successor. The opposition, known as the Fronde, became so threatening in 1649 that young Louis XIV and his mother fled Paris. Feeling ran high against all Italians. In 1650, consequently, Della Bella returned to Florence. Here, apart from several trips to Rome, he worked until his death in 1664. For a time he was drawing master to the young Medici prince Cosimo III. Continuing to do work for the Medici, he also depended on his Paris market, sending plates and prints there. In Florence he found time to experiment, producing prints with an effect much like that of the still-to-be-invented aquatint process. One of these is reproduced on page 55. It is reported that he painted, but no oil by him survives.

In these later days he yarned about his adventures. Baldinucci reports hearing him tell of being trapped in a narrow Paris street by armed bullies, Mazarin haters, bent on assassinating him simply because he was recognizably Italian. A woman witnessing the attack cried out, "What are you doing? This young man is not Italian, he is Florentine!" The ruffians stopped for a moment, giving our hero time to declare, "Gentlemen, I am Etienne de la Belle." Nothing more needed to be said. They released him and retired, making gestures of respect.

Most of the prints reproduced in this book are in the collection of the Metropolitan Museum's Department of Prints and Photographs, several the gifts of Burton Emmett, Harry G. Friedman, Mrs. William Greenough, or Robert Hartshorne, the rest purchased by means of the Harris Brisbane Dick Fund, The Elisha Whittelsey Fund, or the Joseph Pulitzer Bequest. Nearly all the rest of the prints are in the author's collection. The majority of the prints appear in facsimile size; particulars on this and related matters will be found in Notes on the Illustrations, page 134.

Della Bella's prints were catalogued by Alexandre Baudi de Vesme and published by him in *Le Peintre-Graveur Italien*, Milan, 1906; his numbers appear in the Notes. A revised edition of de Vesme's catalogue, entitled *Stefano della Bella*, with addenda, corrigenda, biographical essay, and bibliography, all by the present writer, is published by Collectors Editions, New York. This two-volume work illustrates virtually all of the artist's prints, including examples of variant states.

Seeing the present book into the press, I should like to thank the Trustees of The Metropolitan Museum of Art for awarding me the J. Clawson Mills Fellowship that made possible my research on Della Bella. Thanks are also due John J. McKendry, Curator in Charge of the Metropolitan Museum's Department of Prints and Photographs, who fostered this project at its inception, Janet S. Byrne, Curator of Prints and Photographs, for her kind help along the way, and Leo Steinberg, who first encouraged me to collect Della Bella's prints. Thanks also to The Pierpont Morgan Library for allowing me to reproduce the frontispiece of their *Dialogo* by Galileo as well as a drawing by Della Bella, and to The Frick Collection for permission to reproduce a photograph of its Rembrandt painting The Polish Rider.

P.D.M.

Florence

The story begins in Florence, Della Bella's birthplace, capital of the Medici grand dukes and princes who were the artist's patrons throughout his life. Della Bella executed artistic commissions for the Medici during the first decade of his career, and again in the last decade, after he had returned from Paris to his native city. On the preceding leaf he shows a market-bound *contadino* and a well-dressed equestrienne descending the slopes toward Florence, whose familiar landmarks—the Duomo, "Giotto's Tower," and the Signoria—punctuate the skyline.

Della Bella made this portrait of Cosimo III de' Medici and Marguerite-Louise d'Orléans to decorate a Latin discourse published in honor of their marriage, in 1661. The words on the banner liken Prince Cosimo to the cosmos. The putto in the center holds the world, or cosmos, the putto at the left holds one of the *palle*, symbol of the Medici house, and the one at the right holds the Orléans fleur-de-lys.

Gian Carlo Coppola, in his poem *The Universe, or Rather, Italy Triumphant*, utilizes the same pun. The *Cosmo* of his title relates the cosmos to the first, great Cosimo de' Medici, and to the contemporary prince of the same name. Illustrating the action, a warrior in Roman battle dress, bearing the Medici *palle* on his shield, is triumphing over Radageis, king of the Goths. The poem and frontispiece commemorated the heroic Medici past but hardly interpreted the present or foretold the future. By the middle of the seventeenth century the role of Florence as a power in European affairs was about played out.

IL COSMO

O VERO

L'ITALIA TRIONFANTE

To please Gian Carlo de' Medici, his sixteen-year-old potential patron, seventeen-year-old Stefanino della Bella etched this large plate and dedicated it to him. Dated 1627, it shows, in a grand salon of the Pitti Palace, a banquet of the Signori Piacevoli, or Pleasant Ones, a hunting society. For the occasion the salon is decorated with paintings of hunt scenes, dogs are welcome, and the Medici arms are hung with game.

14

· Al Ser.^{mo} Gran Principe Gio: Carlo Medici ·

ri

ol il Conuito fatto dalli Sig: Piaceuoli serui di V. A. S Hò uoluto adombrarlo, con questo mio disegno, & a quell a rappresentarlo, come con la douuta umil
gno me stesso in perpetua seruitù li piacerà con la solita benignità. & grandezza d'animo accettarlo, mentre riuerentemente li bacio la Veste, & li desidero ogni se

AllaSer.ma Princip. Vettoria d'Vrbino Gran Dvc. di Tosc.
Vi dona o Gran Duchessa il suo Ritratto   Polinico al suo tempo il piu stimato
Bernardin Ricci il Tedeschin chiamato   Qui dalla Fama à riuerirui tratto

Bernardino Ricci, called il Tedeschino (the Little German), the favorite buffoon of Grand Duke Ferdinand II de' Medici, presents himself in all his finery, superbly mounted; in the verses below he dedicates this portrait to Vittoria della Rovere on the occasion of her marriage to Ferdinand, in 1637. A putto displays the combined Medici and Della Rovere arms. In the background: Florence. Ricci explains his nickname, acquired in childhood, in his book *The Little German, or Defense of the Art of the Cavalier of Pleasure*. The high point of a banquet for illustrious visitors in his native town of Camerino was the serving of a large pie, and from this he appeared, clad in German costume, to general delight.

Perhaps for the amusement of the Medici, perhaps for sale to the public, Della Bella made two prints of rebuses. Both take the form of an *écran*, a screen with a handle used to shield the face when one sat near an open fire. The prints were meant to be cut out and pasted onto such fans. The lines of this one present Tuscan proverbs about luck or fortune. From the top down:

> *Fortuna e dormi*
> If you're lucky, you sleep
>
> *Ogni [unghia] uno balla a cui la [aquila] Fortuna suona*
> Everyone dances for whom Fortune plays
>
> *Chi ha la [ala] fortuna ogni tantin di chiave, basti*
> For him who has luck, any little turn of the key is enough
>
> *Ognuno sa navicar quando fa sol [do, fa, sol] e vento*
> Everyone knows how to sail when there is sun and wind
>
> *Migliore [miglio re] è un' oncia di fortuna che due libbre di sapere [sa pere]*
> Better an ounce of luck than two pounds of wisdom
>
> *Più fortuna che seno [senno]*
> More luck than sense

16

IL NINO FIGLIO
TRAGEDIA

The Medici were related by marriage to most of the royal families of Europe. In honor of themselves and their relatives, their court and Florence saw lavish spectacles: carrousels, entries, pageants, theatricals, banquets, funerals. Fortunately, an illustrated book often recorded such events. This frontispiece for Gregorio Belsensi's *Il Nino Figlio (The Darling Son)* takes us into a seventeenth-century theater, probably that of the Duke of Modena, to whom the play was dedicated; his arms appear on the proscenium. An audience of courtiers awaits the rise of the curtain. The orchestra is just visible in the pit.

Here is the balletic finale of a play in another theater, Margherita Costa's *Li Buffoni (The Buffoons)*. Della Bella's figures recall those of Jacques Callot, but they are more individualized and less caricatured.

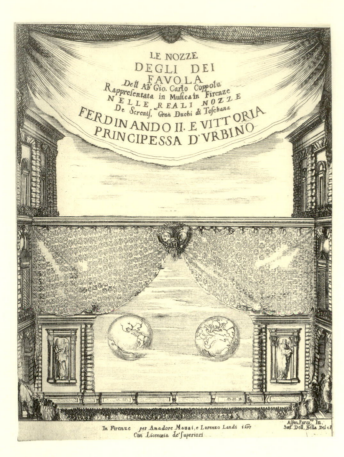

Le Nozze degli Dei (*The Wedding of the Gods*), an entertainment by Gian Carlo Coppola, was staged on July 8, 1637, as part of the celebrations for the Medici-Della Rovere marriage. A temporary theater filled the grotto end of the Pitti Palace courtyard, and the wings of the palace can be seen at the sides of this frontispiece to the souvenir book. The production, which lasted four hours, was choreographed and staged by Alfonso Parigi, one of the prolific family of Medici court artists responsible for decorations on state occasions.

The most splendid of Parigi's effects occurred in the finale. The painted architectural panels at the sides of the stage (present in the frontispiece) were removed, painted cloud drops were lowered to cover the supporting columns, and the widened stage became one vast sky. Twenty-four dancers performed at stage center. Amoretti, flanked by celestial choirs, pranced on clouds above. Still higher, cavaliers cavorted ankle-deep in cloud (actually supported by the terrace atop the grotto at the end of the courtyard). Highest of all floated the Olympian gods, upheld by stage machinery. In the side spaces, beneath the choirs, more dancers spelled FO for Ferdinando and VA for Vittoria. (Shades of today's half-time football shows!)

20

SESTA SCENA DI TVTTO CIELO

Here, Della Bella shows the beginning and end of the second scene of *The Wedding of the Gods*. The curtain opened to reveal Diana, surrounded by her nymphs, celebrating a successful stag hunt. Then Mercury appeared, informing Diana that Jupiter had chosen her as his bride (an episode not shown). Rejecting the offer, Diana had to make a graceful exit. Fortuitously, a cloud rose from a trap in the stage, and the goddess and her nymphs mounted it and floated heavenward. According to a contemporary account, the cloud and its cargo were seized by a strong wind and driven upstage, an action presumably unintended.

SECONDA SCENA SELVA DI DIANA

In April, 1652, Archdukes Ferdinand Karl and Sigismund Francis and Archduchess Anna of Austria (sister of Ferdinand II de' Medici) made a state visit to the d'Este court at Modena. A tournament in costume was staged in celebration, and Della Bella was apparently sent there to make etchings for the souvenir book. The theme of the event was the Four Seasons, and their personifications, along with large replicas of the Austrian arms, surmounted the temporary theater in the palace courtyard. Della Bella here pictures the grand entrance of the participants, accompanied by Aeolus rising in a horse-drawn chariot on a cloud—an effect

made possible by the stage machinery of Gaspare Vigarani of Modena (who later on worked in Paris for Louis XIV). The ensuing mock combats were marred by an accident: Count Montecuccoli fatally pierced one of his friends with his jousting lance.

One of the figures executed by the costumed riders and torchbearers before the Modena combats began.

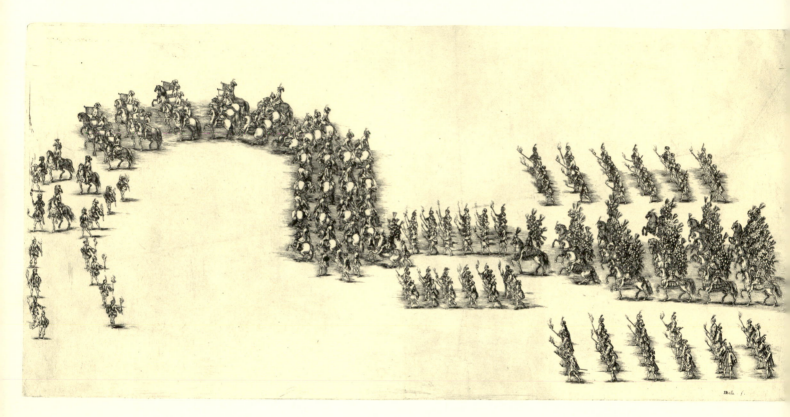

And here, in the same performance, tumblers perform an Italian specialty: *la tombolata*, or *la giuoca della contadina*. Forming pyramids, they pose, or march along, then somersault to earth, their gymnastic feats enhanced by the carrying of blazing torches.

Naue del colonbo gia Trasformata da Nettunno in Orca Marina, et ora da Proteo ritornata nella
sopra essa Andar al Conquisto del Oriente Per l'Augustᵐᵃ C

ua Forma con l'ordina.za de Caualieri che deuano
[u]ustria

ΙΧ.44·.

When Ferdinand Karl and his party reached Florence, another horse ballet and tournament was staged. This is the
parade of the participants in the Pitti Palace amphitheater
the night of April 28, 1652. The foreground float is "the
ship of Columbus formerly transformed by Neptune into a
marine monster, and then returned by Proteus into its first
form." If this seems a little mixed, mythologically, it gave
splendid opportunity for theatrical machinery. The marine
monster issues from a grottoed mountain topped by the
Austrian double eagle. Beyond the amphitheater, its banks
of seats crammed with spectators, are the Boboli Gardens
and the Belvedere Fortress.

NEXT PAGE:

Della Bella's last illustrations for a Medici souvenir book
record *Il Mondo Festeggiante* (*The Celebrating World*), a
festival staged in 1661 in honor of the marriage of Cosimo
III de' Medici and Marguerite-Louise d'Orléans. Again the
performance is in the Pitti Palace amphitheater. Atlas has
circled the arena and taken his place at the center. His
sphere, the world, will open to disclose four girl singers,
and after their song Atlas will change into a mountain.
These effects required the services of an engineer, Ferdinando Tacca. Prince Cosimo himself, costumed as Hercules
and flanked by torchbearers, rides past below, left of center.
Following the parade, Cosimo joined his bride in the box at
the far left to watch the rest of the entertainment.

27

Comparsa del Ser.^{mo} Principe di Toscana Figuran.^{do} Ercole Accompa.^{to} dai Carri del Sole e della Luna, e segu

Il Sig.^r Alessandro Carducci In.^{re} del Ballo e Battag.^{ia}
Nel Teatro Congiunto A

Caualieri d'Europa America. Asia ed Affrica Nella Festa a Cauallo Rappres.ta Per le Reali Noze dell A.S.S.ma
O.   Del Ser.mo G.D.   Fen.do Tacca Ing.re

Ordinanza Nella, quale Si fermarono li Ser.mi Prin.pi Le Squadre de Caual.ri ed Icarri delle Deita intorno al monte d'Atlante nella Fesla a Cauallo Rappre.ta Per le Reali Noze dell A.S.S Nel Teatro Cong.te al Pala.zo Del S.G.D

In this second view, framed by the shadowed wings of the palace, Atlas-become-mountain stands between chariots representing the sun and moon. The cavaliers, in four groups, were costumed to symbolize Europe, Asia, Africa, and America. The light of many torches was supplemented by the flaming pyramidal towers fed by "Adriatic waxes" (probably naphtha and asphaltum). "The shadows of the night were made as resplendent as the brightest day," reported one witness.

In the wooded hills north of Florence were the villa and gardens of Pratolino, designed by Bernardo Buontalenti and constructed during the years 1569–86. The commissioner was probably Francesco I de' Medici, great-uncle of Grand Duke Ferdinando II and Gian Carlo. The buildings and grounds reflected Francesco's known interest in "the competition of nature and art." In Della Bella's day the villa still served the Medici princes as a hunting lodge.

Nature and art were combined in a remote corner of the grounds. Surrounded by an octagonal enclosure, this ancient oak provided a haven of cool shade enhanced by a fountain at its roots and water jets spurting at intervals along the wall. A rustic double spiral stair gave access to a dining platform in the branches.

Art vied with nature inside the villa, which had several grottoes on its lower floors. Della Bella employed a "double exposure" to show the hydraulic automatons at either end of this one. At the left a seated Pan plays his pipes. According to an old description, he also rose and chased the listening Syrinx. At the right—the opposite end of the grotto—Fame flaps her wings while a peasant holds out a cup of water to a thirsty dragon. Facing the entrance in both views is a fountain embellished by a statue of a river god symbolic of the Mugnone, the river that watered the Pratolino gardens and operated the mechanical figures.

"A place for wild nature, surrounded by mountains and full of woods," wrote Francesco de' Vieri in one of the earliest descriptions of the villa (1586). Della Bella found the setting substantially the same when he made his etchings sixty-odd years later. At the end of a forest path the Grotto of Cupid enticed the visitor, though he risked a dousing on the way to it, thanks to the assiduous *fontanieri* who operated the surprise jets and sprays.

NEXT PAGE: Terminating the north axis from the villa, a crouching giant personified the Apennine Mountains. The statue still exists, but the grotto behind it has tumbled down, and the rooms inside the colossus have lost their frescoes of men mining precious ores.

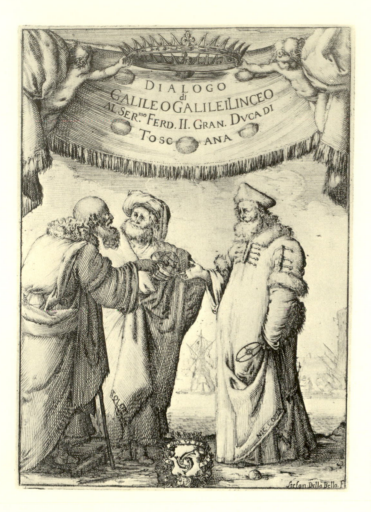

Official Medici commissions to illustrate books linked Della Bella to some notable Tuscans. Galileo, under the Medici aegis (symbolized in this frontispiece by the Grand Ducal crown and the *palle* on the banner), was able to pursue his research in Florence, despite papal disapproval, during the years 1616–32. One result was this book of 1632, the *Dialogo*, in which Galileo reiterates his theories of the movement of the earth and the fixed position of the sun. Expecting to be received into the august company shown here—Aristotle, Ptolemy, Copernicus—Galileo was instead forced to recant his proved truth under threat of torture by the Inquisition. He published nothing more.

The Tuscan saint Andrea Corsini, not widely known even in Della Bella's day, was canonized in 1629, but successive plague years delayed publication of the commemorative book until 1632. Since Della Bella undoubtedly etched the plates the year of the *festa*, they are among his earliest works. The frontispiece shows the barren façade of Santa Maria del Carmine draped for the canonization ceremony.

SVPER ASPIDEM ETBASILISCVM AMBVLABIS

"*Upon the asp and basilisk shalt thou tread*"—Psalm 91. Della Bella portrays another Tuscan saint, Giovanni Gualberto, serenely standing upon these symbols of the devil. The illustration is from a life of the eleventh-century saint, published in 1640. In the background is the abbey of Vallombrosa, near Florence, founded by Gualberto in 1073.

FRANCISCVS EX PRINCIPIBVS ETRVRIÆ.

One of the duties of a Medici court artist was the illustration of funeral books. From such a book comes Stefano's posthumous portrait of twenty-year-old Francesco de' Medici, apparently after an oil portrait by Justus Sustermans. The painting, now in the former royal apartments at the Pitti Palace, shows the young man full length, in blue steel armor. Francesco had left Florence at eighteen to learn the military art under the great Wallenstein, commander of the armies of Francesco's uncle, the Holy Roman Emperor, Ferdinand II of Austria. An early sacrifice in the carnage of the Thirty Years' War, Francesco died of the plague at the siege of Ratisbon in 1634.

Another illustration in Francesco's funeral book shows Brunelleschi's somber church of San Lorenzo with an overlay of macabre decorations for the obsequies. These embellishments were designed by Alfonso Parigi, whose other duties for the Medici included the staging of theatricals (page 20).

38

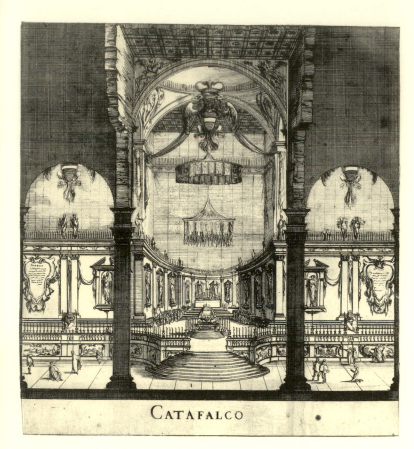

CATAFALCO

Three years later Parigi decorated the same church for the memorial service honoring Ferdinand II of Austria, the Emperor. Della Bella's foldout illustration in the commemorative book cuts away the nave wall and arcade to show a broad view of the transept, the catafalque beneath the dome at the crossing, and the principal altar beyond. The double eagle of the Holy Roman Empire, the shield of Austria on his breast, hangs above the catafalque.

This drawing by Della Bella, probably done on the spot, roughs out the ideas detailed in the print.

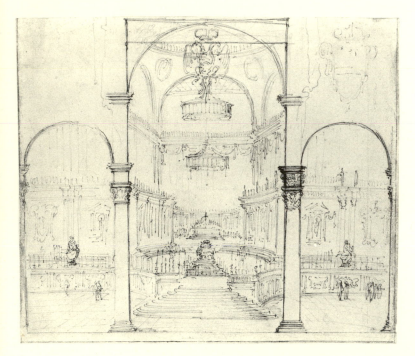

Rome

When Stefano was in his twenty-third year his dearest wish was realized, for his patron Don Lorenzo de' Medici made it possible for him to go to Rome, goal of most ambitious young artists. Drawing there from antique statuary was considered the best possible artistic discipline. In the print below, made later in Paris for a set teaching drawing techniques, Della Bella acknowledged his debt to Rome by portraying the spirit of Drawing, crowned with the laurels of fame, among the ruins of the Forum.

While living in Rome Della Bella indulged his passion for sketching in the Campagna. Here, one sees him at work, surrounded by vestiges of Roman monuments and watched by a shepherd.

S. D Bella inuent. et fecit /   A Paris chez P. Mariette, rue S. Iacques a l'Esperance,   Auec priuilege du Roy   1

12

NEXT PAGE: *The Entry of the Polish Ambassador*

Most ambassadors to the Holy See regaled the populace and honored the Pope with a grand entry into Rome—often staged weeks after their actual arrival. On November 27, 1633, George Ossolinsky, the ambassador of King Ladislaus IV of Poland, marshaled an impressive cavalcade, consisting of Polish aristocratic landlords and their retinues, plus the retainers of other national and native groups. The entry began at the Piazza del Popolo, and the terrain shown by Della Bella at the start seems to be that of the Porta del Popola, just north of the Piazza. Good reporter that he was, Stefano must have been up early to sketch the costumed riders and caparisoned mounts while they were assembling.

The six prints of the set make a strip over eight feet long. Lettered legends beneath the prints identify the various groups.

A. 2 Polish couriers dressed in satin with velvet jackets
B. 22 mules decorated in various styles
C. Light cavalry of the guard of His Holiness
D. Mules of the Lord Cardinals
E. Ten camels with the most splendid saddlecloths of embroidered red velvet, with shoes, headstalls, and headbands of silver, led by Persians and Armenians in diverse dress
F. Four trumpeters with jackets of green velvet
G. Thirty archers dressed in red satin with bows in hand and muskets slung
H. Page at arms dressed in gold brocade in Persian style

44

m giubbe di velluto uerde
G. Trenta Arcieri vestiti di raso rosso Con archi in mano, e carabine pendenti
H. Paggio d'Arme vestito di Brocato d'oro alla Persiana

nee con Selle ricchissime di lana d'oro le due prime tempestate
Archi Freeze Mazze Scimitarre et altr Arnesi di guerra con Briglie gioielate
L. Mastro di stalla di S.E con bel Abito è mazza d'Argento in mano
M. Venti Camerieri di S.E vestiti di Damasco di color d'Acqua marina

I. Twenty pages of His Excellency dressed in aquamarine on an orange ground

K. Five Turkish horses decorated with heron plumes and various jewels, with the richest saddles of gold lamé, the first studded with diamonds, the third with rubies, the two last ones with turquoises, laden with bows, arrows, maces, scimitars, and other weapons of war, with jeweled bridles and shoes of gold

L. Stable master of His Excellency with a beautiful suit and a mace of silver in hand

M. Twenty servants of His Excellency dressed in aquamarine damask

N. Various Spanish Lords and Gentlemen sent by Cardinals and other Ambassadors

O. Many Polish Knights with costumes and horses of great value armed with silver maces

P. There follow other French Cavaliers and Cavaliers of His Holiness

N. Diversi Signori Spagnoli, e Gentilhuomini mandati da Cardinali, et altri Ambasciatori

O. Molti Cavalieri Pollacchi con Abiti, e Cavalli di gran valore armati di Mazza d'Argento

P. Seguiva altri Cavalieri franzesi, e Camerieri di S. Santità

Q. Other Polish Nobles accompanied by Roman Princes and Nobles

X. The Most Excellent Ambassador with costume of iridescent gold lined with precious furs clasped with jewels with a large hat with jewels and plumes of the most exquisite beauty on a graceful steed with shoes, bridle, and stirrups of jeweled gold, accompanied by the Archbishop of Amasia and the Patriarch Gaetano and other Prelates of the Court followed by many Polish footmen together with the Swiss Guards of His Holiness

Y. And afterward the carriage of His Excellency of green velvet pulled by six Persian horses with other carriages

Q. Altri nobili Pollacchi accompagnati da Principi e Titolati Romani

46

O.   *Molti Cavalieri Pollacchi con Abiti e Caualli di gran valore*   P.   *Seguiua altri*
       armati di Mazza d'Argento

L'Eccellentiss.º Ambasciatore con Abito d'oro cangiante foderato con pretiose Pelle affibbiato d'Gioielli conBerrettone   Y.   E doppo la Carozza di S.ª di
con Gioiello e Pennachio d'esquisita bellezza sopra vago Corsiero con ferri briglia e staffe d'oro gioiellate accompagnato dall'   vestito verde tirata da sei Caualli
Arciuescouo d'Amasia e Patriarca Gaetano et altri Prelati della Corte seguito da molti staffieri Pollacchi insieme con la Guardia della Squiccere di S. Santita   Persiani con altre Carozze

These individual horsemen may have been part of Ossolin-sky's display at Rome in 1633, or they may have appeared in a similar entry made into Paris on October 29, 1645, when Ladislaus IV was seeking the hand of Marie-Louise de Gon-zague in marriage. Della Bella has supplied characteristic backgrounds for these likenesses.

An African light cavalryman is armed with bow and javelin. In the distance an elephant lumbers along in a battle train.

S. D. Bella. F.   Cum Privil. Regis.

A Polish hussar, carrying a battle hammer, rides with his traditional feathered wings attached to his back. At H. in Ambassador Ossolinsky's entry is another of these winged riders.

A Moor, armed with bow and javelin, rides an Arabian horse with leopard skin beneath his saddle. Palms, a mosque, and minarets give the scene authenticity.

Roman Views

Della Bella made many views of Rome in which he combined aspects of the monuments and ruins with vignettes of contemporary life. His Castel Sant'Angelo, etched about 1634, shows the downstream aspect. The conventional view is from the other side of the Ponte Sant'Angelo, which is here at the right. (The bridge received its Bernini angels some years after this print was made.) The flags and smoke from cannons signal an important event: a religious festival, the arrival in Rome of notable visitors, or a military victory.

FACING PAGE: The Colosseum served as a shelter for herds. Its arcades are still used today by carriage drivers seeking cover from sudden showers.

Beyond the group of stallion, mare, and foal Stefano provides an accurate rendering of the north and east faces of the Pyramid of Caius Cestius.

CASTELLO S.T ANGELO

Stef. Della Bella jnuent fecit   F.L.D.Ciartres exc. cum Priuil. Regis Chrst.

Stef. Della Bella jnuent fecit.   F.L.D.Ciartres exc. Cum Priuil. Regis Christ.

Here Della Bella gives us the local color of one of Rome's outdoor living rooms, known familiarly as the Campo Vaccino, or Cow Pasture. Although his perspective dramatizes the setting, his view corresponds to other strictly topographical prints that show the Forum from the Capitol. The foreground structure is the Temple of Vespasian. At the far left is the Temple of Antoninus and Faustina with the church of San Lorenzo in Miranda poking up through it, and beyond it, to the right, the small round church of Saints Cosmas and Damian. Between the half-buried columns in the foreground is the Column of Phocas and beyond, at the far end of the Forum, the church of Santa Francesca Romana (left) and the Arch of Titus (right), the medieval wall of Rome joining them. At the far right is the Temple of Saturn.

After the Antique

Now in the Uffizi, the Medici Vase was still, in the seventeenth century, among the antiquities at the Villa Medici on the Pincian Hill. Stefano's study of this vase and other pieces in the Medici collection is reflected in his ornament plates (pages 69, 70), in which he uses swirling, fat acanthus leaves, heads growing out of lush foliage, and entwined vine leaves and bunches of grapes. Here drawing master Della Bella has set Cosimo III de' Medici, his young pupil, to copying the famous vase.

ROMÆ IN HORTIS MEDICÆIS, VAS MARMOREVM EXIMIVM

The inspiration for the figure above may have been a Penelope, a meditating Electra, or a mourner from a sarcophagus.

In the print above, right, Della Bella carefully reproduces the stylized figures of a priestess and a sacrificial bull from a Roman relief, but renders the woman's hair and facial expression in a natural, human manner. The relief, now in the Uffizi, is thought to have been inspired by the reliefs from the Balustrade of Athena Nike on the Acropolis. This etching is of special interest technically, for here the artist employed a dilute acid process on his plate to simulate the watercolor wash he used frequently in his drawings.

Here again Della Bella uses an antique relief as the starting point for his putto in a mask. The hand signal, while quite possibly as ancient as the relief, is the artist's improvement on his model.

Della Bella's inspiration for this print may have been the
Artemis of Leochares (also called the Artemis of Versailles),
now in the Louvre. The sculptured huntress holds her right
hand high and with her left restrains a deer, much as Della
Bella's huntress does her hound.

Paris

Della Bella must have been dazzled by the Paris he first saw in 1639—by its brilliant court life, by its cafés, by its bustling streets. So distracted was he that it is said he enjoyed the city's delights for months before settling down to work, only then meeting with the print publishers François Langlois (also known as Ciartres), Israël Henriet, and Pierre Mariette, whose financial offers had probably enticed him away from Italy.

We can in fancy suppose the title scene below to be one of the artist's first impressions of Paris. He has included recognizable landmarks: the Louvre at the left with the Pavillon de Flore and the ruin of an ancient defense tower, the wooden Pont des Tuileries (later replaced by the stone Pont Royale) spanning the Seine, and far in the distance the bulky twin towers and slender spire of Notre Dame. The

A PARIS Chez Israel, rüe de L'Arbre sec, au logis de Monsieur le Mercier, Orfeure de la Reyne; proche la Croix du Tiroir.

youth contemplating Stefano's engraved stone is costumed in Spanish style—short breeches, hose, and short boots—the dress of a royal page during the years of Louis XIV's minority.

For size and complexity, one of Della Bella's most impressive achievements is his view of Paris across the Pont Neuf from a point between the buildings bounding the Place Dauphine. Besides the well-known landmarks—the Hôtel de Nevers, the Tour de Nesle, the church of Saint Germain

l'Auxerrois, and, at the center, the bronze equestrian statue of Henri IV by the Florentines Giovanni Bologna and Pietro Tacca—the print provides a microcosm of Paris in transit across the Seine. With a glass one can compile a census of 451 people, thirty-eight horses, nineteen dogs, three donkeys, and one lamb. All but lost in the vast scene, nevertheless all contributing to it, are duelists, men fighting with staffs, brawlers routing passers-by, a tooth-puller making an extraction, sellers of sweetmeats and fruits, falconers, hunters with a pack of dogs, a legless cripple, many begging gypsies (one of them telling a fortune), and a hurdy-gurdy player with an audience. Moving among the splendid carriages is a humble water cart, and back among the market stands at the right is an early Seine-side bookstall.

One of the actors in Corneille's comedy *Le Menteur* (1643) speaks ecstatically of the grandeur of Paris:

"A whole, entire city, built with pomp,
Seems to have sprung by a miracle from an old ditch,
And makes us suppose, by its lofty roofs,
That all its inhabitants are gods or kings."

Della Bella, too, must have been impressed with the new architecture, and his publishers were quick to cater to the demand for prints of it. Looking exactly back to where he took his view of the Pont Neuf, Stefano here honors one of Henri IV's town-planning achievements, the Place Dauphine, with its pink-brick, stone-quoined houses built around the triangular space at the tapering end of the Ile de la Cité. Again he shows the statue of Henri IV. This first monumental mounted figure to be erected in a public square in France was presented to the city of Paris by Marie de' Medici in 1614. One of its two creators, Pietro Tacca, had stood godfather to Della Bella in Florence in 1610.

Here is the Place Royale, now called the Place des Vosges, conceived by Henri IV and begun as early as 1603. Uniform façades of comfortable private houses, built by the lesser nobility and the wealthy bourgeoisie, were linked by an arcaded walkway and surrounded an open space planned for promenades or celebrations. This great town-planning innovation was imitated in Germany, Holland, Italy (Turin), and at Covent Garden, London. The statue is of Louis XIII. The dome of the Jesuit church of Saint Paul—Saint Peter (1641) peeks above the roofs at the left. Long in decline, the Place des Vosges has recently experienced a revival. Many of its houses and shops have been repaired and refurbished, and one can again enjoy a stroll under the arcades surrounding the now tree-planted square.

Della Bella shares this plate with Israël Silvestre, friend and colleague from his earliest Paris days. Silvestre, a specialist in architecture, drew the Palais Cardinal, built in 1633–34 by Jacques Lemercier for Richelieu, and Della Bella added the noisy figure of Fame. Late in 1642, after Richelieu's death, Anne of Austria, regent for the five-year-old Louis XIV, moved here from the gloomy Louvre, and the place was known henceforth as the Palais-Royale.

Veuë et Perspectiue du Palais Cardinal du costé du Jardin, et en suitte celles du Louure, et des Tuilleries de diuers costez, et des autres lieux les plus curieux des enuirons de Paris. Par Israel Syluestre.
A Paris Chez Israel Henriet, rue de l'arbre sec proche la croix du Tiroir au logis de Monsieur le Mercier Orfeure de la Reyne. Auec priuilege du Roy.

NEXT PAGE: It is Corpus Christi Day, 1645, and in the garden of the Palais-Royale an elaborate altar has been built. Sheltered beneath a canopy, prelates approach the stairs. Following behind, in public demonstration of his piety, is the seven-year-old Louis XIV. Behind him walks his mother, shaded, like the king, with a parasol held by a page. It is reported that the boy king aroused admiration for the length of time he knelt before the altar.

The architecture of the temporary structure, Italian rather than French, imitates sixteenth-century buildings on the Capitol in Rome or Roman palaces of the early seventeenth century. The crown, supported by angels high above the host, testifies to the indissolubility of temporal power and divine power. Flanking the altar are tapestries after the Raphael cartoons of Saint Paul Preaching at Athens, the Blinding of Elymas, and the Miraculous Draught of Fishes. Never one to overlook a detail, Stefano also shows the fireworks going off outside the garden and, in the distance, the hill of Montmartre.

S. Della Bella f.

A MONSEIG.ᵣ TVBEVF CONS.ᴿ DV ROY EN SES CONSEILS INTENDANT DE SES FINANCES PRESIDENT

Monseigneur᛫: L'amour que vous auez, pour les choses illustres sestant joint a la deuotion tres-particuliere
aussi extraordinaires comme ces deux qualites vous sont particulieres, iay pris l'asseurance de vous presenter le deseing du
eu le bonheur de meriter vostre approbation, iespere aussy Monseigneur que vous me permettres den donner ce

EN LA CHAMBRE DES COMPTES, SVRINTENDANT DE LA MAISON DE LA REYNE, BARON DE VERT.
que vous portez, au St Sacrement pour luy faire dreſſer des autels dont la ſtucture, et les enrichiſſemens ſoient
dernier, pour vous faire connoiſtre combien je tien a honneur quil vous ait pleu de mën donner la conduite, en laquelle puis que iay
temoignage au public, et de me dire a jamais . Monſeig.^r Voſtre treſhumble, et treſobeiſſant ſeruiteur B. D. Amico .

Once again the artist portrays himself at work, this time far from Roman antiquities, in the domesticated lushness of a Paris park. The imaginary monument piles up trophies and symbols of victory in honor of Louis de Bourbon-Condé, Duc d'Enghien. Parisians had reason to be grateful to this twenty-one-year-old commander, for in defeating the Spanish decisively at Rocroi in 1643, he saved Paris from capture.

Plagued by a deforming disease, Paul Scarron (1610–60) nevertheless established himself as a man of letters. In 1652, when he was almost completely paralyzed, he married the beautiful sixteen-year-old Françoise d'Aubigné, who needed a rich protector. Their salon in the Marais was much fre-quented for its diversions and buffooneries, and on Scarron's death Anne of Austria continued his pension to his widow. Françoise later caught the attention of young Louis XIV, was put in charge of his children by Madame de Montespan, and presently displaced her as the king's favorite, assuming the name of Madame de Maintenon.

In this frontispiece, quite in Scarron's witty spirit, Della Bella shows only the hat, shoulders, and heels of the dwarfed author—who insists in his preface that this is nonetheless a true portrait. Della Bella surrounds him with nine importunate bawds, his muses. Beyond, a coarse Pan is about to play his bagpipe, a plump Bacchus sounds a flute, and Pegasus observes the scene from Mount Helicon.

ÆTATIS SVÆ 31º

LES OEVVRES DE SCARRON
A PARIS Chez Touſaincts Quinet au Palais auec Priuilege du Roy
1649

Stef. della Bella f.

Della Bella received only a few commissions for prints of religious subjects, and most of these were executed during his Paris decade for the publisher Mariette. His Madonnas were perhaps inspired by those of Guido Reni, but the personal touch is predominant. There is less of the divine and more of the human about these mothers and children, notably in the realism of their hair and the softness of their draperies.

Stef. de la Bella fecit   *Cum priuilègio Regis*   *Mariette excudit*

Paris publishers also commissioned numerous sets of ornament prints from Stefano. The inspiration for his friezes came from the often unpredictable combinations of architectural, human, plant, and animal forms of ancient Roman decorations—from triumphal arches, sarcophagi, bronzes, funeral urns, and vases. In the second of these friezes a touching Cupid and Psyche scene, framed with a wreath, is flanked by luxuriant plant-stem scrolls that unexpectedly develop into ardently embracing couples.

Bella inu. & fec.   N. Langlois excud.   Cum Priuil. Regis. 10

Bella inu. & fec.   N. Langlois excu.   Cum Priuil. Regis. 7

70

In these vertical ornament panels Stefano impresses his unique style on the standard ornament vocabulary. The foliated tails of bubble-blowing putti make just the right hanging place for a furry bat. A little boy pets his leopard kitten, unaware that its tail has become a soaring floral scroll. Diana, back to the audience, romps with her prey and her half-leafy dogs.

Stef. de la Bella inuent fecit   3   *F. L'Aaglois alias Ciartres exc. cum Priuil. Regis Christ.*

Fantastic vases, often based on antique bronzes, were perennially favorite subjects with printmakers. Stefano out-fantasied all of them, both in the vases themselves and their exuberant contents.

23.^e regna 18

Pepin le bref.
Chef de la seconde race~
Sage, actif, vaillant, aymant ses
Suiets. jl vainquit les Saxons &
les Lombards, donna aux Papes
beaucoup de terres en Italie, &
dompta Gayfre Duc de Guyenne~

25.^e *simples* 31.^e

Louis le debonnaire.
Empereur Il fut mis
en prison par ses enfans

Charles
le Simple
Il se laissa prendre
prisonnier par
Robert quil auoit
vaincu.

48.^e

Philippe 5.^e dit le long
Il souffrit toutes choses pendant son regne~

49.^e regna 6 ans

Charles 4.^e dit le bel
Prince Sage, et aymant la Iustice.
Il rangea au deuoir Edouard Roy
d'Angleterre, et Louis Comte de
Flandres, lequel il fit condamner
pour felonnie, puis luy rendit
ses terres.

32.^e *Malheureux* 41.^e

Raoul *Louis le Ieune*

Il fit la guerre en
Normandie Guyenne
Lorraine, Italie, et fut
malheureux par tout

Il alla a la terre Sainte
sans fruit. Il repudia
Eleonor et luy rendit
la Guyenne, cause des
guerres auec Angleterre.

45.^e

Philippe
le hardy

grand entrepreneur mais
malheureux. Vespres Sicil.

51.^e

Iean

Il perdit la bataille de
Poitiers et fut pris.

54.^e regna 29

Charles sept.^e
Prince facile, mais bon et resolu dans
l'aduersite. auec son courage et le
secours de la Pucelle d'Orleans, jl
reconquit son Royaume sur les
Anglois qu'il chassa de France,
et joignit a ses conquestes la Guyene
et la Normandie.

Fearful of repercussions against him for his administration of France during Louis XIV's minority, Mazarin, Richelieu's successor, chose to keep the boy in ignorance, allowing him scant instruction save in religious matters and the arts of war. Except for an illustrated religious volume, the only "book" permitted the seven-year-old king were four sets of

40.ᵉ — regna 29

Louis 6.ᵉ dit le gros.

Sage, vaillant. jl deffit pres de
Gisors le Roy d'Angleterre et plusieurs
François rebelles. l'Anglois suscita
l'Empereur contre luy, mais il se le
rendit amy, en l'accordant auec le
Pape. jl vangea sur les Flamans
la mort de leur bon Comte, et en
establit vn autre

5.ᵉ — regna 30.

Clouis le grand

Vaillant, sage, Jnfatigable. il
fut le premier Roy de France
Chrestien. jl chassa les derniers
Romains des Gaules. jl conquit
la Guyenne et la Bourgogne,
dompta les Allemans, et s'estant
emparé de toutes les Gaules,
leur donna le nom de France.

10.ᵉ — regna 44.

Clotaire 2.ᵉ

Juste, moderé & vaillant.
Pendant son bas aage Fredegonde
Sa mere, et la mechante Brunehaut
firent mille maux, mais depuis
leur mort Il pacifia Sagement
Son Royaume.

Saincte

Anne d'Austriche

Reyne de France, Saincte, Sage, d'vne
bonté merueilleuse, et d'vne modestie
pareille a sa grandeur. Petite fille
d'Empereurs, fille et sœur de deux grands
Roys, femme d'vn plus grand encore
et tousjours victorieux, et mere d'vn
Roy donné du Ciel a ses vœux, qui
surpassera tous les Roys du monde.

21.ᵉ — regna sous les feneants.

Charles Martel

Vaillant et sage, il fut esleu par les
Estats Prince des François. il def=
fit pres de Tours Abderame auec
quatre cens mil Sarrasins, il les
deffit encore en vne seconde ba=
taille. il dompta les Frisans et
les fit Chrestiens. Quelques vns ne
le comptent pas entre les Rois.

playing cards, devised by Jean Desmarets de Saint-Sorlin
and etched by Della Bella. Through simple games with these,
played perhaps like Authors, Louis acquired at least a
smattering about geography, mythology, history's famous
queens, and the kings of France—good, bad, and unfortu-
nate. The monarch himself, crowned, sits beside his mother
on the card of Anne of Austria.

Vertumnus and Pomona

Ceres (Demeter)

The fall of Phaethon

Actaeon

Salmacis and Hermaphroditus

Jupiter and Danae

Despite their miniature scale, these cards from the Jeu des Fables (reproduced here without legends, in their actual size) present the mythological stories beautifully and originally.

Hercules and Deianira

Jason

Perseus and Andromeda

Pyramus and Thisbe

Cephalus and Procris

Pallas and Arachne

75

Arion

Narcissus

Apollo and Daphne

On the Road

Ifrael excud. cum priuil. Regis.
9.

From Florence to Rome and back again, then from Rome
to Paris and back again to Florence—Della Bella traveled
most of it on horseback, fording rivers, galloping on the
open stretches, climbing over mountains. Though his bag-
gage was limited, there was always room for a parchment-
bound sketchbook. The drawings and quick sketches the
artist made on these journeys provided material for many
series of his prints.

Israel excudit cum priuilegio Regis. 3

A romantic episode on the road in night and storm? More probably this is a trial piece for a book illustration showing Clovis, the first Christian king of France, carrying off his bride, Clotilde. It was she who converted Clovis to Christianity, after he rescued her from imprisonment by the usurper of her father's throne.

Here the storm is real, and the travelers have no shelter from it but their voluminous cloaks.

Stef. de la Bella jnuent fecit   AER   ex. Cum Priuil. Regis Chrift.

S. D. Bella jn. et fe.

Ifrael ex. cum priuil. Regis

From his travel sketchbooks Della Bella produced numerous vignettes of people and places. On this page he gives us a kind of seventeenth-century *Sunday Afternoon at the Grande Jatte:* French folk enjoying themselves on a riverbank. Having costumed her child, a young mother encourages him to dance to the music of an itinerant violinist.

Right: Doubtless a common scene during the Thirty Years' War—a frightened boy giving directions to the breastplated leader of a troop of cavaliers on their way to the next skirmish. below: Gossips at a river crossing trade the latest news.

Israel ex. cum priuil. Regis

Stef. della Bella.

S.D. Bella in. et fe.

Israel ex. cum priuil. Regis

A beggar woman, perhaps a gypsy
or camp-follower, burdened with
three lank-haired children—

In these capricci Della Bella gives us more of his travel
impressions:

Savoyards or gypsies
entertaining at an inn
with hurdy-gurdy and triangle—

Peasants discussing crops, the weather, or the war while the old horse rests—

The resting wives, babes, and dogs of a party of gypsies or shepherds—

Pilgrims on their way to Rome, or possibly to shrines in Spain.

A washerwoman makes her way to a riverbank on a fine morning.

Louis XIV began riding lessons at seven; at nine he was considered an amazingly good horseman. The favorite game of the king and his playfellows—sons of counts, dukes, marshals, ministers of state—was war. To train the boys for eventual generalship, Mazarin ordered built in the garden of the Palais-Royale a miniature fort, with sturdy walls, moat, bastions, and cannon that fired blank charges. Louis and his *enfants d'honneur* practiced cavalry charges, marched to drums, and beseiged the fort. These four small prints, from a set of nineteen dedicated to one of Louis's young companions, illustrate the techniques of good horsemanship.

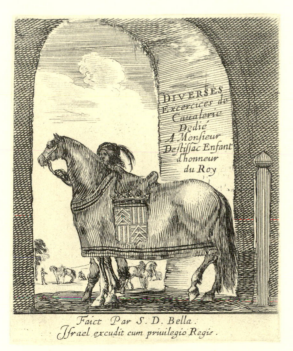

The schooling of horse and rider that prepared both for the exigencies of the battlefield.

The artist catches the heat of battle in a cavalry combat of Rubensian fury.

Perhaps because he was with the French forces, and thus reporting from the winning side, Della Bella emphasizes the action in his prints of war and plays down the miseries, in contrast to the aspects shown by his predecessor in the field, Callot.

RIGHT, ABOVE: There is at least a hint of melancholy, as, the fighting over, a weary battle train leaves the field.

BELOW: In more routine reportage an officer supervises the operation of a battery firing on Arras during the siege by the French in 1640. The man touching off the piece stands as far from it as possible. Kegs of powder are being brought up for the next round, and an armored swabber stands by.

Varij Capricij Militarij di Stef. Della Bella 1
P. Mariette le fils excudit Cum Priuilegio Regis Christ.

S.D. la Bella fecit *F.L.D. Ciartres excud. Cum Priuil. Regis*

Della Bella's reporting included either observed or imagined sea battles. BELOW: The end of a fray between Christians and Turks, Turks swimming at the right while another in the shallop shoots an arrow. RIGHT: Beset by galleys, a galleon desperately fires its cannon.

NEXT PAGE:

In 1640 the city of Arras, in the north of France, was occupied by the Spanish. Sent by Richelieu himself to "cover" the French siege, Della Bella was on the scene in June, his presence there documented by his dated sketches in the British Museum. His large plate of the siege, made in Paris in 1641, combines three views. In the center is a maplike plan of the city's defenses, made as if from a mountaintop, the star-shaped fortified walls indicated at the center, within the outer defense walls and the deployed forces of the defenders and besiegers. Depth and versimilitude come from the detailed foreground picture of the French moving upon the city. At the top, on a *trompe-l'œil* scroll, is a ground-level view of the city, with a skirmish in progress.

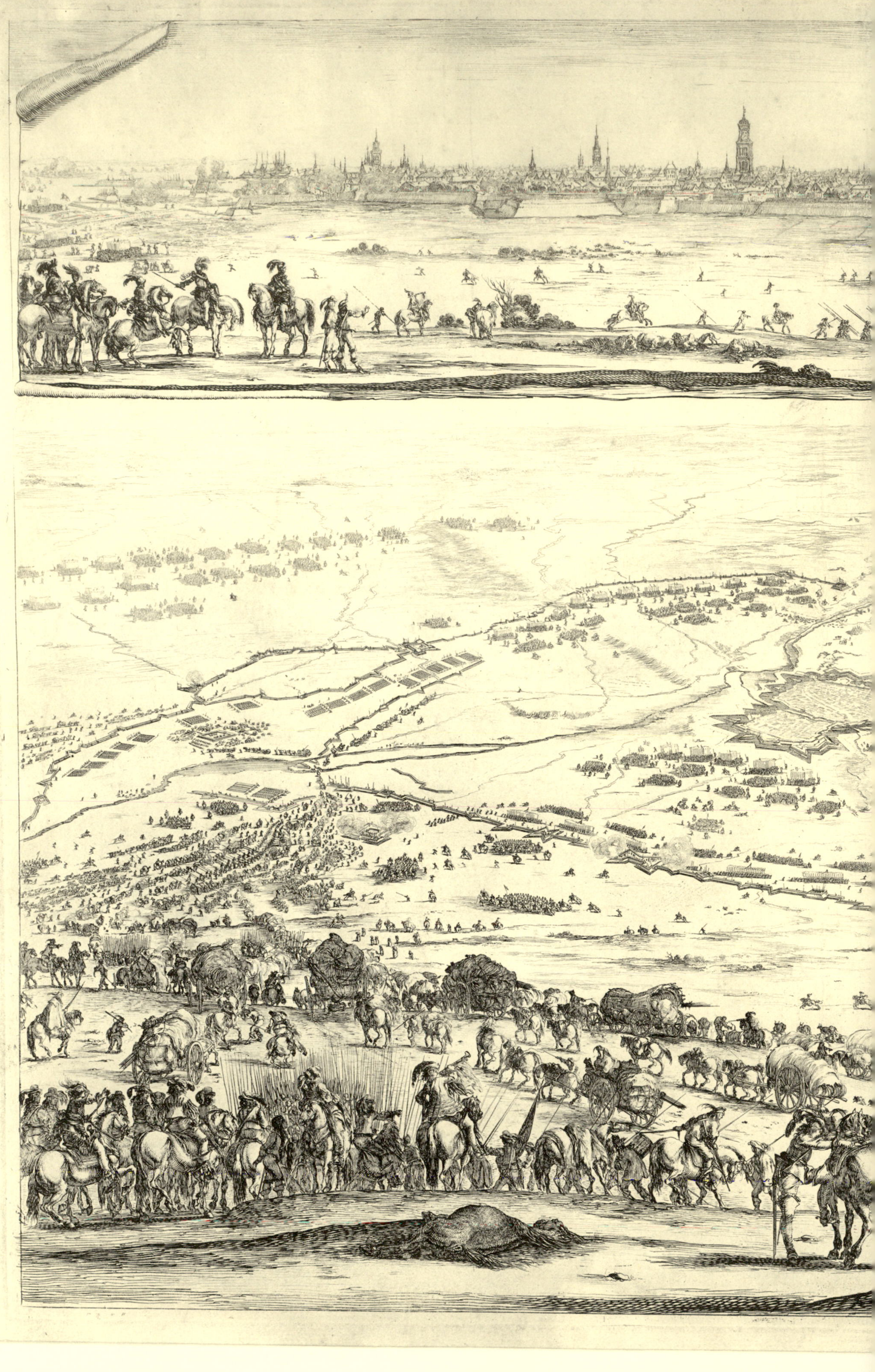

Plan der Belagerung v. Arras. Anno 1.197. Welt. 88 b. No. 5x.

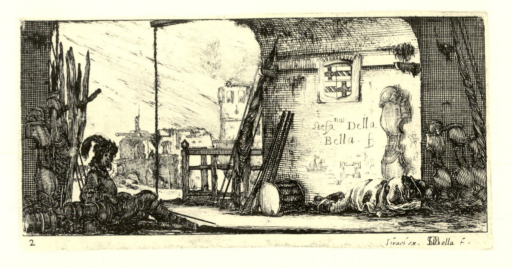

The subjects of this set—artillery transport, troop movements, cavalry clashes, attacks upon towns—came from Stefano's experiences before Arras, that city recognizable in the last of the selection shown here (page 98). These etchings are among the finest in Della Bella's œuvre. The career of the Conte de la Roche-Guyon, the dedicatee of this set of 1644, is summarized in three notices in the *Gazette de France*: May 19, 1643, fought at Rocroi; June 1644, wounded at siege of St. Philippe; August 13, 1646, killed at Mardick.

4

SBella F.

5.

Israel ex.   SBella F.

6

SBella F.

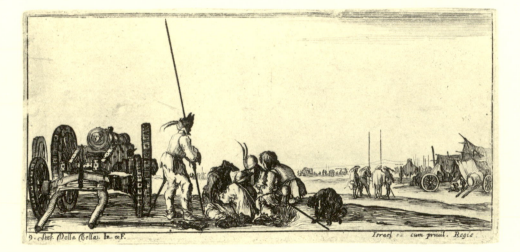

Landscape

A large number of Della Bella's surviving drawings testify to his lifelong interest in outdoor sketching. Sometimes he set himself the problem of translating accurately into prints his light pencil sketches or his drawings made with fine-point pen and light wash. His answer, seen below and in the print on page 102, was an etching technique of unique fineness and lightness.

Although most French and Italian printmakers of the seventeenth century could hardly equal the quantity and quality of Dutch landscape prints, Della Bella showed unexpected talent in landscape and produced many sets for his Paris publishers. In Paris he certainly studied Dutch prints, particularly the work of Herman van Swanevelt and Jan Both. In his vertical landscapes, done in the 1650s, Stefano's adaptation of Dutch techniques is evident in the large format and use of a painterly style. The tonality is darker and denser than in the earlier marines and capricci, the skies are no longer blank, and the plant, animal, and human forms are treated less schematically.

We are not so much aware of the art in these prints as we are of enjoying the landscapes for themselves: the light and shade, the prevailing weather, the people and animals on the move or at rest.

Israel excud. cum priuil. Regis
10.

Once thought to represent a stage machine in some court pageant, this fantasy landscape of Mount Parnassus is now known to be an illustration for an allegorical thesis in celebration of the Chigi who became Pope Alexander VII. Philosophers, two of them laurel-crowned, converse in the foreground. Further back, soldiers surprise Archimedes, and Diogenes is seen in his barrel. Other philosophers slowly climb Parnassus to the glory of the gods above its summit. With its six *monti* and star, the mountain symbolizes the Chigi crest.

After the grandeur of Parnassus, the serenity of the Roman Campagna with its herdsmen and their flocks and the remains of ancient tombs.

Stef. Della Bella inuent fecit

F.L.D. Ciartres exc. cum Priuil. Regis Christ.

6   Stef. della Bella fecit   Cum priuilegio   Mariette excud.

Stefano made many drawings and prints of animals, particularly exotic ones. Sketchbook sheets of camels could be useful, as for the set of heads, left, or perhaps for a biblical scene. Stefano certainly encountered camels when he sketched the train of the Polish Ambassador at Rome, but he may have known them even earlier in Florence, for Ferdinand II tried to establish camels in Tuscany as beasts of burden.

4   Stef. della Bella fecit .   Cum priuilegio   Mariette excud.

The lion, bear, and boar are from a set of twenty-four animal prints. The creatures Stefano did not encounter in pastures or while hunting he probably sketched in court menageries.

19   Stef. della Bella fecit   Cum priuil .   Mariette exc.

16   *Stef. della Bella fecit*   *Cum privilegio*   *N Langlois ex.*

From the diary of Giacinto Gigli, May 1630: "*In this month was brought to Rome an Elephant animal, which formerly for a hundred years had not been seen, one of which was sent as a gift from the King of Portugal to Pope Leo X in 1514. But this one belonged to a private man, who also managed it that, whoever wanted to see it, had to pay one giulio.*" Presumably the beast also got to Florence, and Stefano drew it there.

From the frequency of the subject in his output, and from the descriptive accuracy, Della Bella must have hunted himself, possibly with his Medici patrons in the preserves around the villas of Pratolino and Poggio a Caiano. Like a stop-action cameraman he has here frozen the flight of a doe and prodigiously etched her every coarse, short hair.

Although there were ostriches in royal and ducal menageries in Italy and France during the seventeenth century, it is unlikely that they were ever plentiful enough to hunt. This chase was doubtless imagined—along with the palms that look strangely out of place on the grassy Tuscan hills. Stefano again shows his technical virtuosity, this time in the painterly rendering of the bird's fluffed-up feathers.

In Stefano's landscape roundels it seems as natural to find sporting satyrs, young and old, as it is to see a cowgirl and her cow at a fountain.

Ste. Della Bella in. et fe.   Cum Priuil. Reg.

A drover—perhaps, by his dress, a rural god—moves his herds down a slope toward a river ford.

S.D.Bella inu. & fec.   Cum Priuil. Regis

By the Sea

Della Bella was apparently fascinated by seaports, perhaps because of his inland upbringing. Besides, marines were popular, so he etched several sets of them, large and small. By his Paris days he had found his style and could abandon the static figure-posing of his first marines. He fills these later ones with realistic action and detail. ABOVE: Wind, weather, and a raking light give color and life to the scene.

The six prints following are from a set including views of Amsterdam as well as the stormy strait between Calais and Dover. It has been cited as evidence for a visit by Della Bella to Amsterdam in 1646 or 1647. And indeed the depiction of Dutch housefronts, canal barges, and the Herringpacker's Tower is convincing. Stefano's topography is as correct here as it is in his Roman views, and it cannot be said with certainty that he made use of others' prints of Amsterdam. The next step is tempting: "Della Bella visited Amsterdam, ergo he visited Rembrandt." But if they met, neither spoke the other's language. There is evidence that each artist took something from the other, but the medium of exchange was probably prints, not conversation.

Veue d'Amsterdam.

Autre veue d'Amsterdam.

Veüe d'vn coin de Calais

Tour de Calais.

116

S. D. Bella *inuenit et fecit*   Veuë des Coftes d'Italie.   Ifrael ex. cum priuil. Regis.

A Paris, Chez Ifrael, rue de l'Arbre fec, au logis Mônfieur le Mercier, Orfeure de la Reyne pres la croix du tiroir.

Livorno

Cosimo I, Francesco I, and Ferdinand I de' Medici created the fortified harbor of Livorno and made it the port for the Tuscan navy. The Knights of Santo Stefano, a military order established in Livorno by Cosimo I, were dedicated to liberating Christians held by pirates or Turks and propagating the Christian faith.

In the print below a galley departs, watched by townsfolk and two Turkish merchants. A statue of the Virgin watches over the ship's company from the poop.

Stefano shows here, surrounded by waterfront activities, the marble monument to Ferdinand I, who completed the port of Livorno. The designer was Giovanni Bandini; the sculptor of the bronze slaves was Pietro Tacca, an artist mentioned earlier (page 62). The bronze for the slave figures came from captured Turkish cannons. The monument stands in Livorno today.

Death

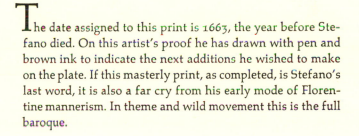

The date assigned to this print is 1663, the year before Stefano died. On this artist's proof he has drawn with pen and brown ink to indicate the next additions he wished to make on the plate. If this masterly print, as completed, is Stefano's last word, it is also a far cry from his early mode of Florentine mannerism. In theme and wild movement this is the full baroque.

Icy la Mort triomphe entre les funerailles;
Ses plus beaux promenoirs sont les lieux des batailles;
Son Throsne s'affermit de la cheute des morts;
Elle change a l'instant par ses armes subtiles
En riuiere de sang les Campagnes fertiles,
Et les plaines de Mars en montagnes de corps.

Ste. Della Bella in. et sc. Cum Pri. Reg.

Parmi les Escadrons, elle fait des rauages
Du trenchant de sa faux, s'ouure mille passages
Caualiers et Cheuaux tombent egalement,
Et ses coups sont si prompts, q'vn puissant corps d'armée
D'vn milion de corps horriblement formée
Semble n'auoir laissé q'vne ame seulement.

Death on the battlefield, death by the plague—both were familiar to Della Bella. Paris's children and women are the victims of these rushing, screaming deaths. In the first two prints the background is the walled Cemetery of the Innocents. The topography is so accurate that Della Bella surely must have sketched in this terrifying place, for centuries virtually the grave of all Paris. The ground was strong here. Bodies rotted quickly, and skulls and bones were then moved to open cribs over the arcades around the walls. The pebbles in this earth were teeth.

Epilogue

Della Bella and Rembrandt

Della Bella as a Source for Other Artists

Rembrandt's The Polish Rider, in The Frick Collection, wears the *joupane,* or long fur-lined coat, that originated in the Near East and was common to Poles and Hungarians in the seventeenth century. His fur-lined hat is an ordinary European type. He carries two swords, one curved, the other straight, a bow, arrows, and a battle hammer, the latter in use throughout western Europe. Costume and accouterments mark the man as a mercenary light cavalryman, one who hired himself out to various commanders all over Europe during the Thirty Years' War. Della Bella published his series of exotic riders (see also pages 48–49) in 1651, basing his subjects either on his drawings of the entry of the Polish Ambassador in Rome (1633) or the similar entry in Paris (1645). The art historian Julius Held has pointed out that Della Bella's riders were very probably known to Rembrandt and used by him as material for his painting, which was done about 1655. Della Bella is known to have bought Rembrandt etchings, and his presumed trip to Amsterdam in 1646 or 1647 may have included a visit with Rembrandt. Could the two have exchanged work, or did Della Bella send his set of riders to Rembrandt as a present?

S. D. Bella. F.

Cum Priuil. Regis.

S. Rossi inu. & fec.

Cum Priuil. Regis.

Della Bella's prints were a bountiful source for artists in the field of decoration. This drawing of a clock, by an anonymous eighteenth-century French hand, adapts the putti and goat motif from one of Della Bella's large etchings.

When Pierre Moreau, in the mid-eigh-
teenth century, made his print of fantastic
architecture with a pyramid, it was easier
for him to make use of a Della Bella print
of a camel than to go afield and sketch a
living one.

NOTES
ON THE ILLUSTRATIONS

Prints marked PDM in the following list are in the author's collection; the rest, except as noted otherwise, are in the Metropolitan Museum's Department of Prints and Photographs. Where given, the dimensions (in millimeters) are those of the complete original print. They appear only when the reproduction in this book is either larger or smaller than the original or where less than the entire print is reproduced. In the latter case, a small image of the entire print is appended. On page 141 are the inscriptions that have been cropped from beneath some of the reproductions, notably the mythological subjects on pages 74–76.

PAGE	DE VESME CATALOGUE NUMBER		DIMENSIONS	
2	757	Title sheet (detail), *Diverses Paysages*. (See below, page 66)		

Florence

PAGE			DIMENSIONS	
11	783	Equestrienne nearing Florence	243 x 185	
12	37	Cosimo de' Medici and Marguerite-Louise d'Orléans	135 x 135	
13	959	Frontispiece, IL COSMO		
14–15	43	Banquet of the Piacevoli	253 x 380	
16	39	Bernardino Ricci	360 x 252	
17	689	Rebuses on theme of fortune		
18	961	Frontispiece, IL NINO FIGLIO		
19	933	Frontispiece, LI BUFFONI	185 x 129	
20	918	Frontispiece, LE NOZZE DEGLI DEI	193 x 147	
20–21	924	Scene six, *Le Nozze Degli Dei*		
22	920	Scene two, *Le Nozze Degli Dei*	198 x 288	
23	51	Amphitheater, Modena	550 x 421	
24	62	Cavaliers in Modena performance	240 x 495	
25	63	Tumblers in Modena performance	322 x 225	
26–27	66	Ship of Columbus, Florence		
28–29	71	*Il Mondo Festeggiante:* entrance of Cosimo III		PDM
30	70	*Il Mondo Festeggiante:* Atlas as mountain	275 x 435	PDM
31	838	Pratolino: ancient oak	246 x 360	
32	841	Pratolino: views of grotto	246 x 360	PDM
33	842	Pratolino: allée with water jets	240 x 365	PDM
34–35	843	Pratolino: colossal statue		PDM
36	905	Frontispiece, DIALOGO DI GALILEO GALILEI	201 x 14	Pierpont Morgan Library
	884	Saint Andrea Corsini	148 x 113	
37	929	Saint Giovanni Gualberto		PDM
38	36	Francesco de' Medici	173 x 120	PDM
39	74	Funeral of Francesco de' Medici		
40	77	Service for Ferdinand II	237 x 227	
		Drawing for De Vesme 77		Pierpont Morgan Library

Rome

PAGE			DIMENSIONS	
41	834	Arch of Constantine and Colosseum	305 x 267	
42	364	Frontispiece, PRINCIPII DEL DISEGNO	120 x 158	PDM

134

43

51

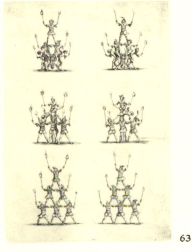

63

842

834

757

On the Road

821

837

692

797

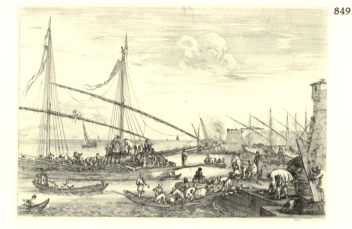

849

87

Death

Epilogue

DELETED INSCRIPTIONS

783 Chez M.r Vincent proche S.t Benoit ruë St Jacques à Paris. SDBella

933 LI BUFFONI COMEDIA RIDICOLA DI MARGHERITA COSTA ROMANA

51 SDBella

63 SDBella

842 SDBella

74 SDB

834 Arcus Const.ni et Amphit.ri Flavij Panetinae

835 Templi Concordie inter Capito.um et forum R. reliquiae. (Actually, this is the Temple of Vespasian)

498 *Vertumne et Pommone*
Vertumne qui se changeoit en toutes formes, estant amoureux de Pōmone, deesse des fruits, se changea en vieille pour la voir dans son jardin, et l'ayant fleschie se fit cognoistre et en jouÿt.

499 *Phaeton*
Ayant voulu conduire le char du Soleil son Pere, alla trop haut et trop bas, et brulant le Ciel et la terre, fut foudroyé par Jupiter.

508 *Salmacis et Hermaphrodite*
Salmacis nymphe aymant le bel hermaphrodite fils de Mercure et de Venus, se jetta dans le bain ou il estoit, et l'embrassant fit sa priere qu'ils ne fussent faits qu'un corps, ce qui fut fait.

538 *Ceres*
Fille de Saturne, cherchant Proserpine sa fille, et ayant soif, une femme luy donna a boire; et un enfant se moc-quant d'elle fut changé en un Serpent nommé Stellion.

493 *Acteon*
Fils d'Aristée et d'Autonoé, aymant la chasse, trouva Diane dans le bain, qui le changea en cerf, et il fut devoré par ses chiens.

539 *Jupiter et Danäé*
Jupiter amoureux de Danäé fille d'Acrise Roy d'Argos, qui l'avoit enfermée dans une tour d'airain, se changea en pluye d'or et descendit dans la tour; ou il joüyt de Danäé qui enfanta Persée.

511 *Hercule et Deianire*
Hercule fils de Jupiter et d'Alemene ayant espousé De-janire, pria Nesse le Centaure de la passer une riviere, lequel estant avec elle au dela de l'eau, la voulut ravir. hercule le tua d'une flesche.

515 *Jason*
Fils d'Eson Roy de Thessalie, alla en Colchos avec les Argonautes, et conquit la toyson d'or avec l'ayde de Me-dée, ayant endormy le dragon qui la gardoit. il s'enfuit avec elle, qui depuis estant repudiée tua leurs enfants, et s'enfuit sur un char tiré par des dragons.

514 *Pyrame et Thisbé*
S'estant donné rendezvous dans un bois pres d'une fon-taine, Thisbé vint la premiere, et se cacha voyant une Lione, et ayant laissé son voile que la Lione ensanglanta, Pyrame croyant que la Lione l'eut devorée, se tua, et elle trouvant Pyrame mort se tua aussi.

537 *Persée et Andromede*
Andromede fille de Cephée et de Calliope ayant esté exposée a un monstre marin, Persée retournant avec la teste de Meduse qu'il avoit tuée, la vit, tua le monstre et espousa Andromede.

540 *Cephale et Procris*
Cephale voulant tenter la pudicité de Procris sa femme, se desguisa et la corrompit. Elle l'ayant recognu senfuit dan les bois dont il eut regret, et l'ayant priée de revenir elle luy donna un chien et un dard inevitable, dont il la tua depuis.

536 *Pallas et Arachné*
Arachné Lydienne est tres-scavante en l'art de tapisserie et de broderie, deffia Pallas en cet art, et en ayant esté surmontée elle se pendit. Pallas la changea en Araignée.

541 *Arion*
Excellent musicien fut jetté dans la mer par des mar-chands pour avoir son bien, et ayant joüé de sa lyre avant que d'estre jetté, un dauphin le receut et le mit au bord.

502 *Narcisse*
Fils du fleuve Cepluse et de la nymphe Siriope, estant extremement beau, devint amoureux de luy mesme en se mirant dans une fontaine, et mourant de regret de ne pouvoir joüir de son amour fut changé en une fleur.

501 *Apollon et Daphné*
Daphné poursuivie par Apollon, fit un vœu a Diane, qui la changea en laurier. Apollon s'en couronna tousjours depuis, et c'est l'arbre vas Vainqueurs et des Poetes.

DATE DUE